Brigitte and Gilles Dellu

DISCOVERING LASCAUX

Photographs by Ray Delvert
Translated by Angela Moyon

SUD OUEST

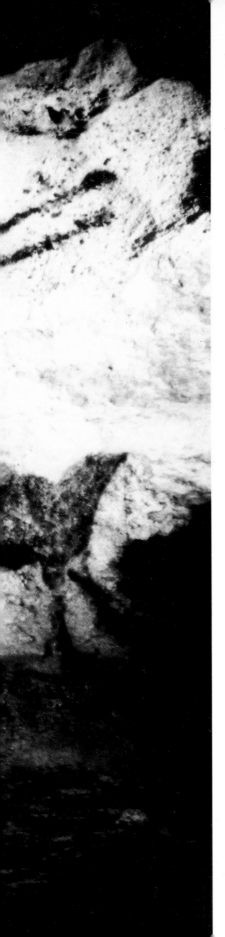

The Vézère Valley,
The dawn of the Magdalenian Period,
The reindeer and a few other The Cro-Magnons, creatures...

The cave at Lascaux is an extraordinary coming-together of a country, a moment in time, animals and men.

And this is no doubt what makes this decorated cave unique.

1 — Bulls' Chamber. The «unicorn» (L = approx. 7 ft.) thickly outlined in black. A composite animal (the body of a rhinoceros, the withers of a bear or bison, the head and spots of a big cat, and the tail of a horse), or an imaginary drawing of a feline as described in the oral tradition. Two horses lightly drawn in red on the body. To the right is a brown horse (the head was rubbed away by a falling splinter of rock). This enigmatic «unicorn» is the first large drawing seen when you enter the cave.

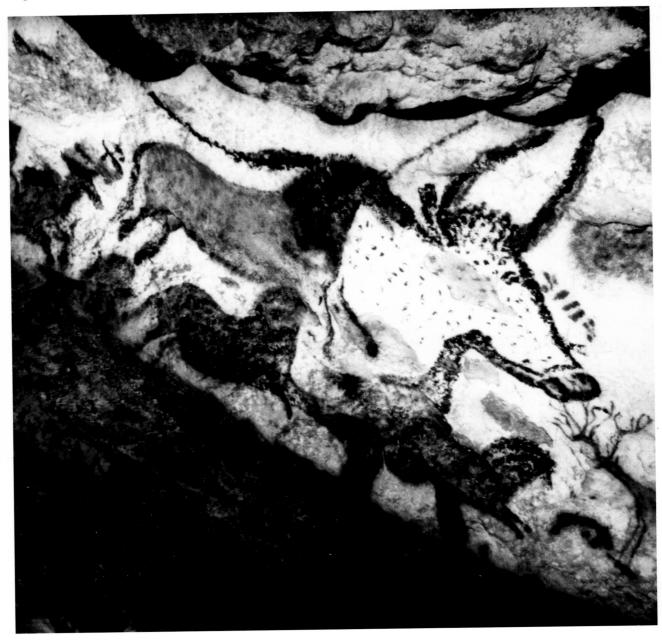

*2 — **Bulls' Chamber.** The first large bull, or aurochs (L = approx. 10 ft.) outlined with a thick black line. The horns and withers are highlighted in red. Beside the bull is a large red horse with a black head, and a row of small brown horses.*

*3 — **Bulls' Chamber**. A red horse with black head (L = approx. 6 ft. 6 ins). The ears are perked up and the head is small in comparison with the remainder of the body. The short legs are thrown forwards and backwards in a contrived «canter». The front left leg is detached from the chest by a twist of perspective.*

A country

THE VEZERE FLOWING BETWEEN HILLS AND CLIFFS

At this point along its course, the black river, still full of marl and mica from the borders of Corrèze and pebbles from the Limousin, flows through a wide valley between fields of tobacco and maize, between lines of poplar trees and meadows, at the foot of the gently-rolling limestone hills of Dark Périgord. It is here that Man built Montignac, a traditional little town with the ruins of a castle.

The Vézère of Corrèze, further upstream, flows for miles through the narrow gorges of the cristalline rocks in Limousin. Downstream, beyond Thonac, it gouges out a difficult, grandiose passage through the limestone of Le Moustier, La Madeleine, and Les Eyzies between cliffs riddled with caves and rock shelters. This river is both a major route in and out of the area and an artery on whose banks human settlements have existed for the past 200,000 years.

Its tributaries are modest waterways, no more than a few streams, most of them dry cums slicing into the plateau, dividing it into a myriad of small uplands, hills or mounds, some bare, others covered with a few trees. One such is the hill at Lascaux, on the left bank of the Vézère.

In Dark Périgord, limestone predominates, forming cliffs, rocks, haughty roques, gritty slopes, and uplands hidden in some places beneath a thin covering of earth or sand. This is Coniacian, a yellow rock rich in iron, which reddens when exposed to heat. It is coarsegrained, and as full of sand particles as it is of limestone. It is broken up by a small number of faults but most often, it is cracked by diaclases that open the way for the underground streams which gouge out the countless caverns.

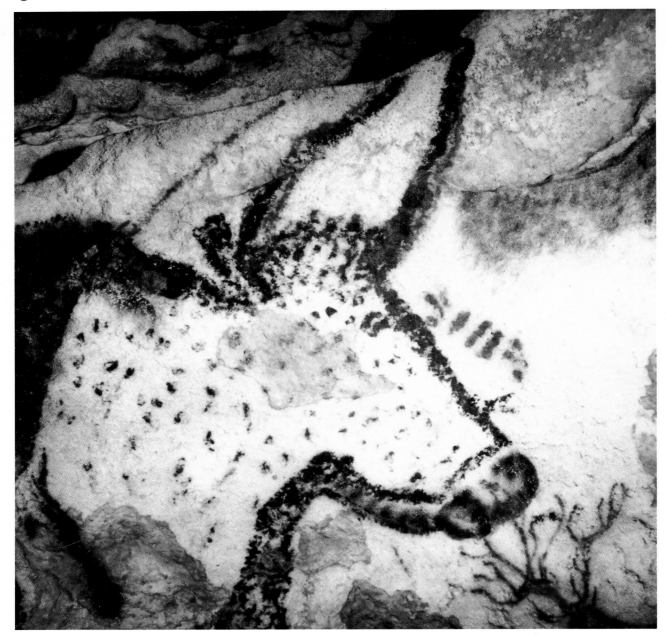

4 — Bulls' Chamber. The head of the first large bull (photo 2). The horns are set on the top of the head, to each side of the striped tuft of hair. The eye is depicted by means of two lines. The white muzzle is separated from the cheek by a curved line. The head and neck are dotted with black spots. There is a symbol in front of the head consisting of short red lines.

5 — Bulls' Chamber. *The head of the second large bull (photo 9), which faces the first one. The horns are shown from three-quarter view (one is C-shaped and the other forms an S), which is a typical way of portraying perspective in Lascaux. The ear is set onto the nape of the neck. The tuft of hair on the head is depicted by two parallel lines. There are dots around the eye. Between the two bulls is a red horse, with no legs. It has a brown body, the mane is fluffy and its ears are perked up.*

*6 — **Bulls' Chamber**. A group of stags between the first two bulls (each stag is just over 2 ft. in length). They have slender heads, a complex set of antlers, and legs thrown stiffly out to the front and back in a rigid gallop.*

A CAVE AMONG THOUSANDS

Périgord is the land of the thousand caves. From the water sinks through which they seep, the rivers make their way underground, vigorously drilling a passage for themselves at the expense of the vertical fractures or the joints separating the horizontal strata in the rock. In some places, the ceiling of the subterranean galleries has collapsed, forming a modest pothole, or «aven». Often these networks of underground passages were later subjected to a invasion by red clay, sand or stalagmites. On the hillsides, some of the entrances have been blocked up. Often, the streams have abandoned the galleries, to run deeper and deeper down in the earth. And so there are the dry, fossilised caves that we can visit today, narrow tunnels with barely enough space for potholers to squeeze through or beautiful spacious caverns, some of which have been laid out to cater for visitors.

Some of the larger caves (less than thirty of them, plus a dozen rock shelters) were decorated by prehisto-

7 — Bulls' Chamber. A brown stag heavily outlined in black (close-up of photo 6). The two antlers (withe double tines) point forwards from the top of the head, a traditional feature of the deer in Lascaux, with one antler pointing vertically upwards and the other slanting backwards. Behind the antlers is a short line that marks the ear. The abdomen has a paler strip. There is no tail. The hooves are oval and elongated with a pointed tip. Above them is a spur. The hooves are divided in two by the frenum of the two cloots as if they were seen from below.

ric man from the Gravettian c. 25,000 years ago until the end of the Magdalenian some 10,000 years ago. The smallest is only a few yards long ; the largest, spreading over several miles, is now equiped with a small underground railway. It is a well-known fact that many of the cave mouths and shelters provided a ready-made awning for the homes, or even the tombs, of Neanderthal or Cro-Magnon man. Yet no prehistoric settlement has been discovered here far below the surface. Cave men did not actually live in caves. At least not in Périgord.

Faced with a choice of a thousand caverns, Cro-Magnon man selected the one on the hill in Lascaux 17,000 years ago as the setting for the most outstanding underground sanctuary in Prehistory. This is one of the largest caves in the area and its walls were the most suitable for painting, engraving and mural art.

There was little merit in man's having discovered this cave. At that time, its porch, the outlet of an age-old subterranean stream dating from the early Tertiary Era lay wide open at the foot of a sheer cliff, amidst a few stunted oaks, pines, hazelnut bushes, and junipers on an sundrenched, arid plateau.

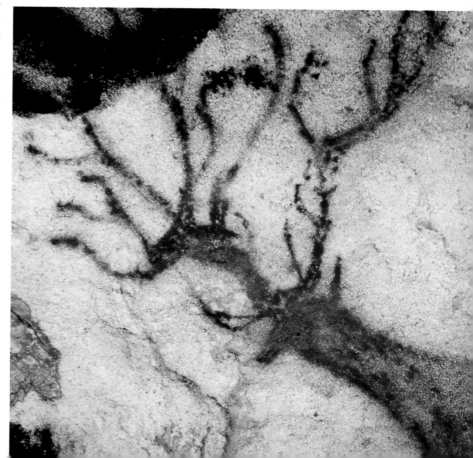

8 — Bulls' Chamber. A red stag with a too lavish, disorderly set of antlers. The ear protrudes from the nape of the neck (close-up of photo 6).

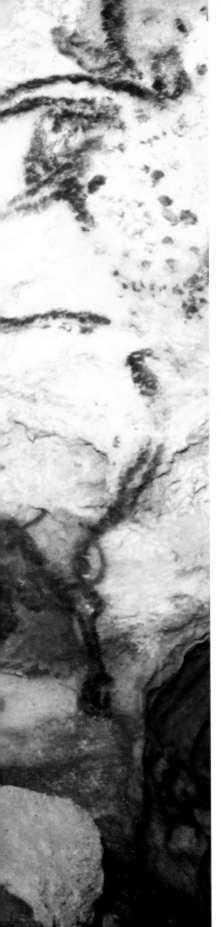

10 —Bulls' Chamber. *A red bison that blends into the line of the belly on the second large bull (photo 9). The head and hump are massive ; the front legs are merely sketched in, forming a V-shape. The horns are depicted in the usual way i.e. the one furthest from the observer is a C-shape, the nearest forms an S.*

9 — Bulls' Chamber. *The second large bull (L = approx. 12 ft.) depicted with genitals and a thick neck. The animal is characteristic of the style used to represent cattle in Lascaux i.e. the head seen in profile and the horns from three-quarters angle, the ear protruding from the nape of the neck, the enormous body seen in profile with the breast seen from three-quarters angle, short legs in motion, and hooves seen from the front (massive ovals separated into two cloots) with a spur above them. The shoulder has a barbed marking. A small red stag overlays the back legs and a red bison overlays the line of the belly.*

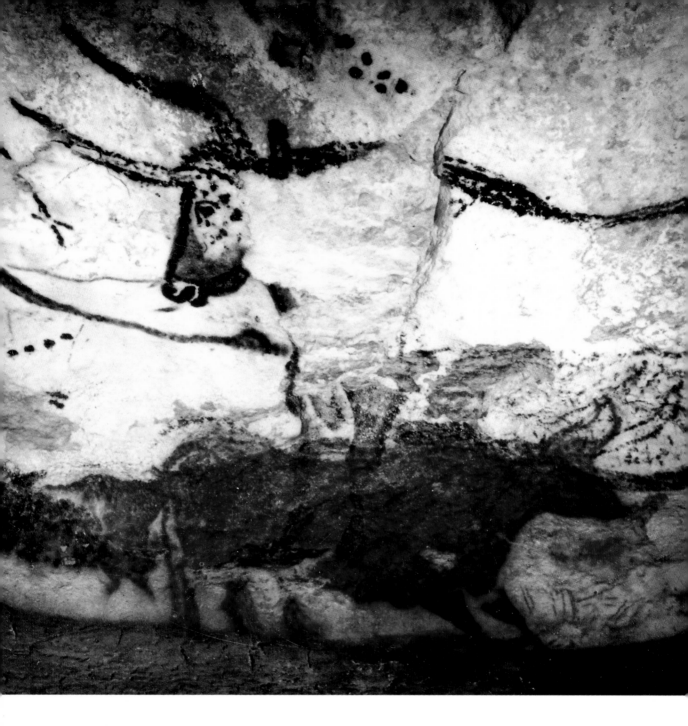

11 — Bulls' Chamber. *The fourth large bull (L = approx. 18 ft.). The breast rises above the hind quarters of the third large bull, partly concealing it (giving an effect of perspective). The head, which has been damaged by a rockfall, has over-sized horns. To each side of the animal are signs`symbols - an oblique cross, a thick line and a row of dots, a rectilinear sign with a barb which seems to have been stabbed into the muzzle, and a small black line in front of the mouth (perhaps representing the animal's breath ?). At its feet, in a position similar to that of the bison shown in photo 10, is a red cow with corns outlined in black, followed by a small red animal that was not completed (it may have been a calf).*

As the visitors advanced into the cave along this fossilised waterway, tallow lamps lit up a vast rotunda (*the Bulls' Chamber*) and a narrow diaclase (*the Axial Gallery*). Grafted onto the side of it beyond a low gallery that can only be visited on hands and knees (*the Passageway*) was the lofty diaclase known as The *Nave*, with its two extensions. To the right is the wider *Apse* containing the *Pit* while at the end is the narrow corridor known as The *Felines' Gallery*. It is a complex layout spread over 250 meters but limited to two main galleries - one forming the entrance (Bulls' Chamber, Axial Gallery) and the other deeper one consisting of the Passageway and Felines' Gallery. The first of these galleries is easy to visit ; the second is steeper, with low roofs on some sections and two small shafts.

First and foremost, though, it was an empty cave. A layer of waterproof marl gave it an impenetrable roof through which the chalky water was unlikely to seep, trickle or run. This cave has none of the stalactites, stalagmites or flowstones (or calcite flows) that usually adorn the walls of Périgord's caves. On the contrary, the undamaged roof and walls, almost totally free of peeling or scaling, are simply covered (in the Bulls' Chamber and Axial Gallery) with an immaculate even layer of calcite, which may have cristallised when the cavity was filled with water in days long gone. The lower sections of the walls are covered with a more clayey substance. In the other passageways, the rough, yellow rock is nearly always bare. The ground consists of clay and sand throughout the cave, although the first chamber contains gours, concretions that were formed by low dams across a temporary stream. The calcite-covered walls of the Bulls' chamber and of the Axial Gallery, entrance, sparkling with small, hard, white cristals were only painted. The engravings and paintings including certain engraved details decorate the walls of the other yellow ochre, siliceous galleries in which the limestone altered gradually, as if changing one grain at a time.

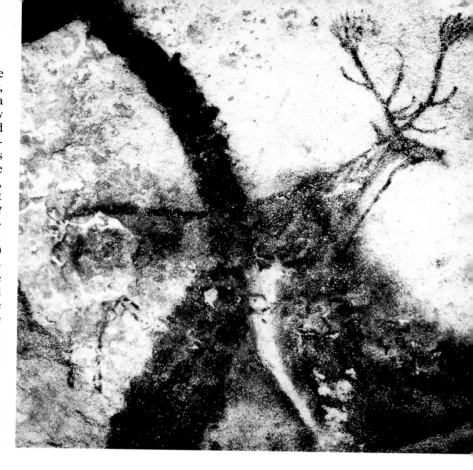

12 — Bulls' Chamber. A stag (L = 2 ft. 4 ins.) crossing the breast of the third large bull. The design and size are identical to that of the stag in photo 7. The tips of the antlers form a strange fan-shaped design.

There was, then, a twofold choice - the choice of this cave rather than any of the many others, and the choice of the technique used for the graphics, which was selected to suit the existing state of the cave walls.

As far as the cave itself is concerned, we have learnt much that was totally unknown to the Magdalenians. The porch of their cave-sanctuary collapsed relatively soon after they left it, following successive periods of ice and thaw, closing off the entrance to the network of underground passages for 170 centuries. In this forgotten microcosm, an independent climate established itself, regulated by almost imperceptible draughts that slowly kept the damp air moving while the low temperature was maintained by a huge conical rockfall. This prevented any condensation on the walls and evacuated the carbon dioxide that was produced naturally.

The artefacts left behind by the painters, engravers and visitors in prehistoric times remained in their places, on the ledges of the walls and lying on the ground where they gradually became buried by layers of grit that fell off the walls, consisting of a thin layer of clay, a thin stalagmite floor or even the thick calcite of the rimstone pools. This archaeological security system was doubly effective because it was sealed by a few inches of sediment in an enclosed cave. And these remains have enabled us to reconstitute the lifestyle of those who once occupied the cave.

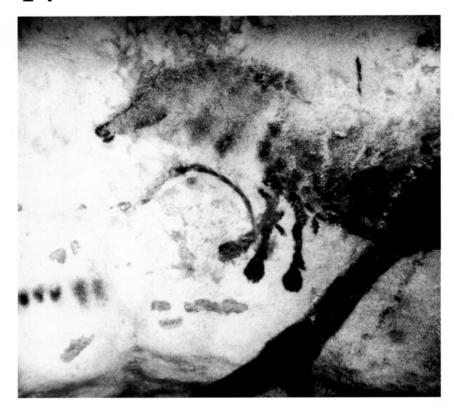

13 — Bulls' Chamber. An unfinished drawing of a horse with three front legs. The animal seems to be emerging from the right front leg of the third large bull and be heading for the Axial Gallery.

ALMOST EVERYTHING TO HAND.

The Magdalenian Period was neither a time of terror nor a golden age. Apart from the shelters provided by its rocks, the Vézère Valley provided the men of Lascaux with stone, timber and animals.

The pigments they required were in the ground - the yellow ochres and browns that reddened in the fire (a mixture of sand and clay, with iron oxyde that was more or less dehydrated), the black manganese (or at least the maganese dioxide) and, even charcoal. The limestone on the hillside could be split into small flakes which made excellent lamps, pallets and crushers for pigments. Flint was fairly common everywhere.

In those days, Périgord had no large forests. Saplings were cut from neighbouring trees to make climbing poles and scaffolding while the bushes provided the vegetable fibre used to make ropes.

There was animal life in abundance - large herbivores, big cats, small animals and birds. Yet it was the reindeer that was most important to Magdalenian man, providing him with food and various materials. This was, indeed, the Age of the Reindeer.

14 — Bulls' Chamber. An unfinished painting of a small three-coloured horse on the shoulder of the third large bull (the head was destroyed by a rock fall). The mane consists of black stripes. Around the animal are numerous stick-shaped signs.

15 — Bulls' Chamber. *A bear (L = approx. 2 ft.) painted in black. The outline blends almost completely into the line of the belly of the third large bull. The head is visible, with its two round ears, as are the narrow muzzle raised expectantly, the protruding withers, the rounded back and the end of one back paw with its claws.*

16 — Bulls' Chamber. A spatter of stick-shaped signs beneath the belly of the fourth large bull (photo 11). Large numbers of geometric signs such as these can be seen in Lascaux, either interlinked to each other or connected with the animals. Their meaning remains a mystery.

17 — Axial Gallery. After the vast Bulls' Chamber, the cave tapers to form a narrow gallery. The top of the walls and the roof are decorated with paintings.

(Overleaf)
18 — Axial Gallery. A red cow with a black head (L = approx. 9 ft). The head and neck are slender, the horns are shown with normal perspective, the body is enormous, the frail legs are in marked perspective and the tail is disproportionately long. The coat is dappled. A paler line follows the line of the back (indicating the coat or merely a second outline ?). The cow is drawn at the entrance to the gallery opposite the large stag (photo 19). Here as elsewhere in Lascaux, the lower section of the rock face, which is rough and dirty, has not been decorated.

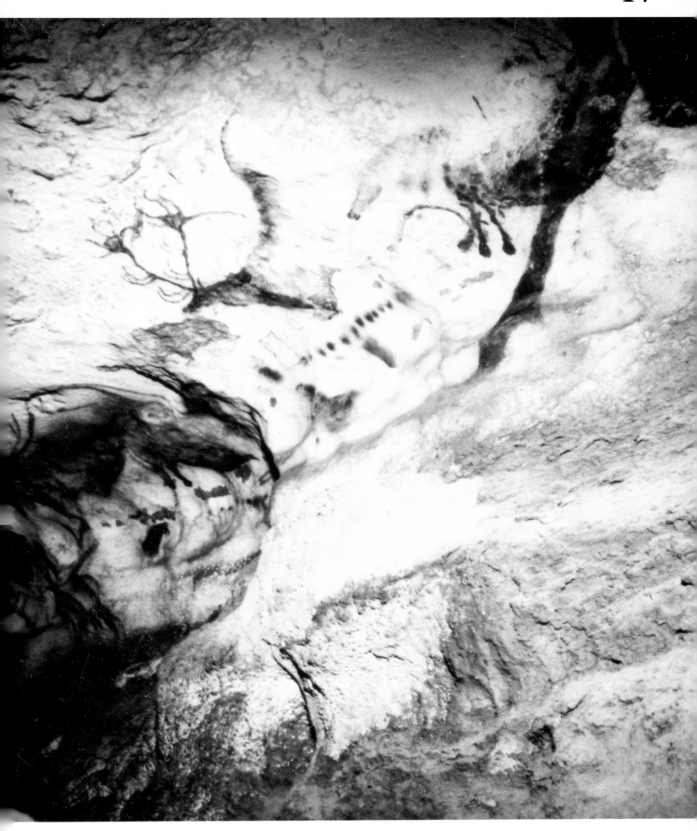

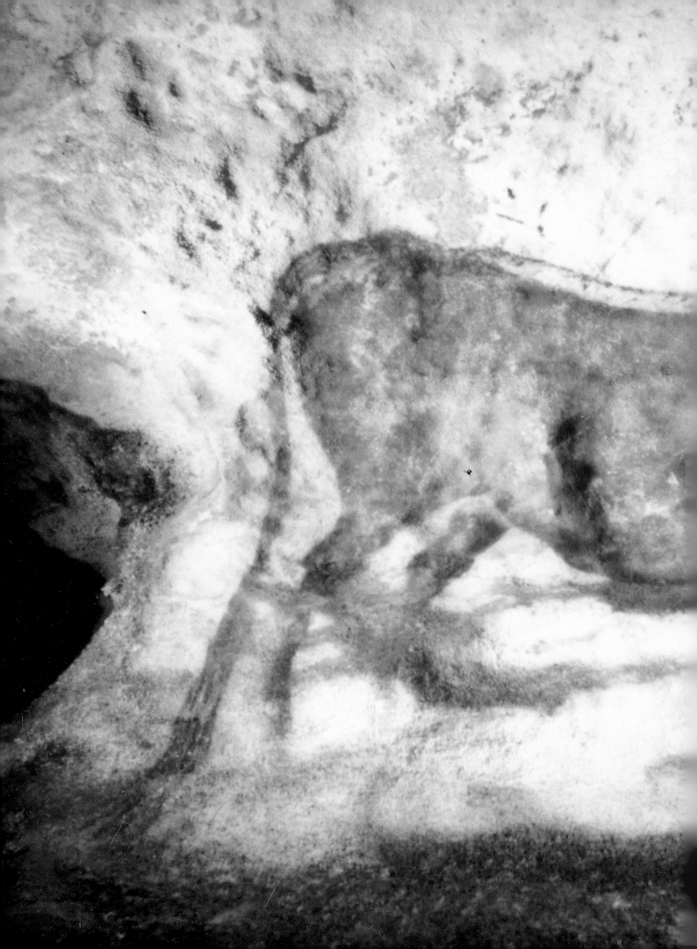

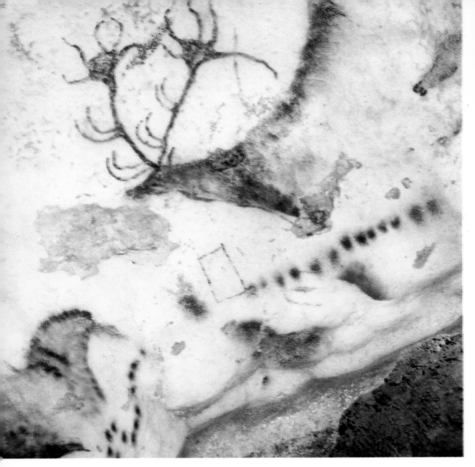

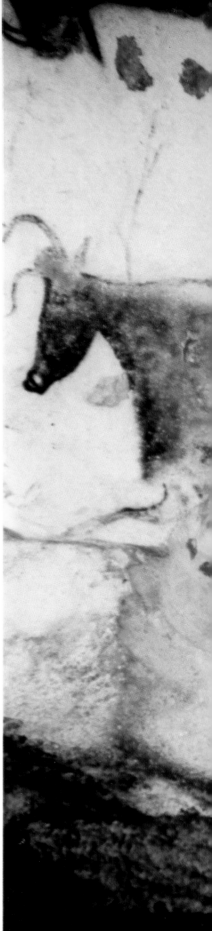

19 — Axial Gallery. *An unfinished painting of a stag with a slender head and pointed ear (Ht = 4 ft. 6 ins). The stag has a mass of antlers with double tines and bays and wide palms bearing the curved tips. Below is a rectangular sign and a row of dots. The stag is flanked by three horses.*

20 — Axial Gallery. *A red cow (L = approx. 8 ft). The front legs are raised while the hind legs merge into the first of the «Chinese horses» (head and neck emphasised by large black dots). In place of the horse's front legs, which are missing, there is a symbol in the shape of a bracket, again consisting of dots. There are numerous signs all around this painting (dots, sticks, crosses, branches).*

(Overleaf)
21 — Axial Gallery. *The two most famous «Chinese horses» (in fact there are six in all, three on each wall of rock facing each other). They are typical of the artistic precepts evident in all the paintings in Lascaux i.e. they have a small slender head, an enormous belly with indications of the coat and two shoulder tripes, short legs shown in movement, and rounded hooves seen from front view. Given the raised front legs on the horse on the left, the photo may well represent a stallion following a mare.*

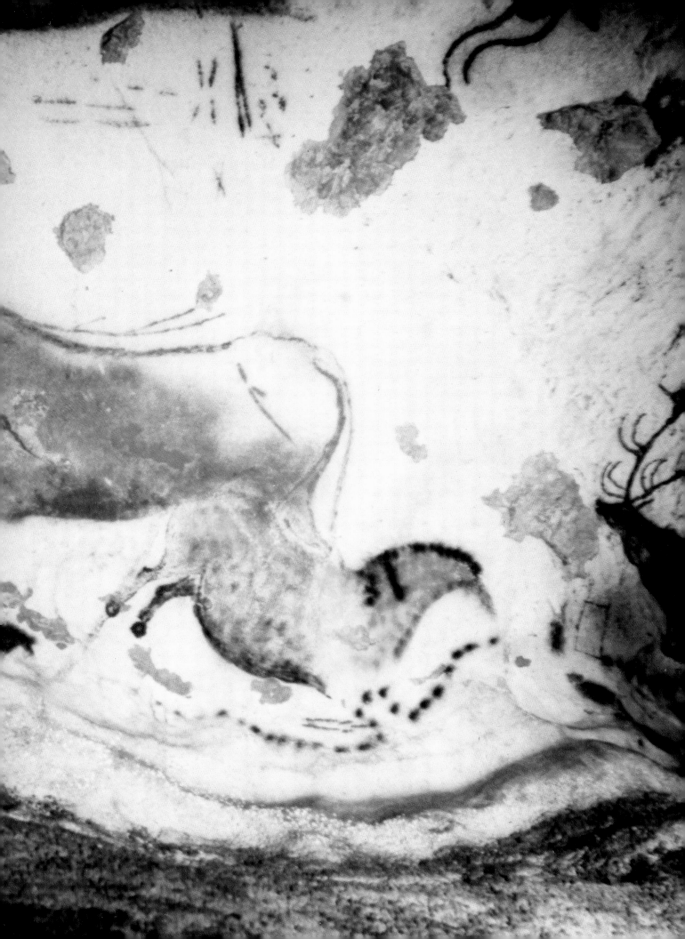

*22 — **Axial Gallery**. A «Chinese horse» in striped winter coat (long hair under the belly). A break in the painting on the front and back left legs adds perspective and emphasises the foreground.*

One moment in time

WITH A FEW GRAINS OF POLLEN.

Flowers die, leaves and wood rot ; but pollen, like all plant spores, resists the passage of time. A durable husk ensures that these microscopic particles, of a shape and size characteristic of each individual species of plant, remain indestructible. For palynologists, they describe the plant environment and, by extension, the climate that was prevalent when the archaeological layer from which they are extracted was first laid down. Examination under a microscope of splinters of wood which have been survived to the present day (this is highly unusual) provide similar information. The appearance of the sediments of each layer on a prehistoric site will also depend on conditions when the deposits were laid down and on the climate.

Cro-Magnon man (like his immediate predecessors, Neanderthal man or Le Moustier man) was subjected to climatic cooling, better known as Wurm glaciation (from 75,000 B.C. to 10,000 B.C.). Yet Europe did not become one vast glacial wasteland. In our countries, although the weather was cooler with annual means of 5°C less than today, man was nevertheless able to live a normal life. Moreover, this climate varied depen ding on the era, the latitude and the proximity of the sea. Such variations had marked consequences on the flora and fauna.

During the period in which Lascaux was inhabited, the climate underwent a fairly humid rise in temperatures which lasted for somewhat less than one thousand years and was preceded and followed by colder periods. This intermediate stage in Lascaux was itself subdivided into various warmer or colder periods. In fact, Lascaux being situated in Périgord, in a geographical location that is equidistant from the pole and the Equator, and from the sea and the mountains, the inhabitants enjoyed a climate very similar to our own i.e. a temperature range of 0° to approximately 10°C in January, and a range of 15° to 22°C in July. Rainfall varied from 500 to 700 mm per year. The winters were fairly long but temperate, the summers were short and not very hot, and the springs and autumns were brief. As for the scenery around the hill at Lascaux, it was not very different (except for the housing and crops) to the landscape before us today.

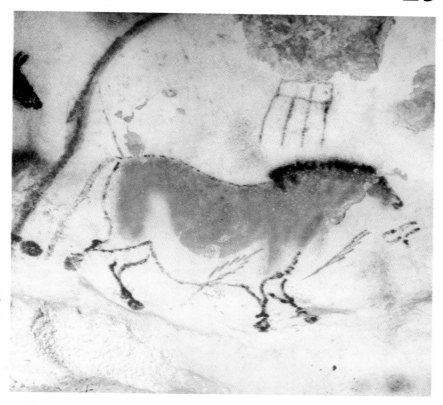

23 — The yellow «Chinese horse» (L = 4 ft. 6 ins) with a pale coat (the breast is highlighted by a natural roughness in the rock). The light M-shaped markings on the belly are common in graphics of the Magdalenian Period. Around the horse are a large number of signs e.g. a quadrangle, a pair of lateral sticks in front of the horse's nose, a line above the hindquarters, and double interlocked chevrons on the breast and belly similar to our own schematic «arrows».

The palynologist, Arlette Leroi-Gourhan, saw the landscape take shape under her microscope. The Magdalenians arrived in the cave during a period of climatic warming and left it as soon as they began to feel the effects of the cold era which followed it. This means that the first inhabitants lived amidst thick forest with hazelnut bushes, pines and tall broad-leaved trees such as oak, lime, elm, ash, hornbeam, and sycamore, beneath which grew privet, currant bushes, black alders and clematis. Here and there, there were even a few trees that demanded a warmer climate (e.g. maritime pines, walnut trees). When the climate became less attractive, the great deciduous trees became more sparse and the countryside was covered in a vegetation that was part tundra (there were more Compositae such as centaury and thistles than Graminaceae, or grasses).

The fauna was such as might be expected in a temperate climate i.e. horses and cattle, deers, ibex, wild boars, brown bears, hares and rabbits, dormice, hedgehogs, frogs and bats. Yet a few species accustomed to colder climes also existed such as the woolly rhinoceros and, perhaps, the musk ox. Most of all, though, there were the reindeer which spent the summer months on the slopes of the Massif Central.

A HANDFUL OF CHARCOAL.

The plant world does not only provide prehistorians with pollen. When charcoal has been preserved, as it was in Lascaux, it can be carbon-dated.

Living organisms, whether animal or vegetable, contain the same proportion of natural carbon (carbon 12) and radioactive carbon (carbon 14) as the atmosphere. When exchanges cease after death, carbon 14 gradually diminishes, in line with a known decrease in radioactivity. Nowadays, measurement of the remaining carbon 14 can be used to determine the exact moment at which exchanges cease.

The charcoal preserved in the one and only archaeological layer of the soil in Lascaux were collected and examined using this method. On average, it is 17,000 years old (to be precise, 17,070 give or take 130 years).

And the objects found in this same layer (flint flakes and spearheads) are of the type used by man at that time (Early Magdalenian).

Animals

INVISIBLE YET OMNIPRESENT : REINDEER

The animal environment of man during the Early Magdalenian Period was dominated by large herds of reindeer. Man hunted them and made use of nearly everything. Yet the animals depicted on the walls in the cave at Lascaux were of quite different species.

The reindeer predominates in this Age of the Reindeer corresponding to the Upper Paleolithic and, more particularly, to the Magdalenian. The animals (ranging from 4 ft 4 in to 7 ft 4 ins in length for a weight of between 1 and 6 cwt.) were migratory and travelled enormous distances. Their main enemies were wolves and,

in summer, the mosquitoes that pursued them from the tundra, pushing them on towards the mountains. Bucks and does had antlers with a long, curved spike at the front. Their head, with a wide muzzle, was low on their chest, their withers were prominent, and they had a long dewlap below their neck. They were large animals (between 8 and 15 hands high) with tendons that cracked slightly at each step. Their feet were wide as if webbed, giving them stability on snow-covered ground. They had a short tail. They ate leaves off trees or other plants and lichen that they nosed out under the snow. At the end of the glacial period 10,000 years ago, they left our country for the polar icecap and nowadays it is very difficult to re-acclimatize them to France.

The reindeer was a sort of prehistoric self-service. The antlers were carved into spears which were then straightened by the addition of other, pierced antlers. The bones were used to make sewing needles and tubes. The hide, with its closeknit covering of hair, was tanned before being cut to make warm clothing and thick mocassins. The tendons were dissected, producing a multitude of sewing threads. The tallow was collected for use in lamps. Then there was the meat, fat, marrow and offal, all of which formed the staple meat diet of the Magdalenians, who varied their menus with berries, leaves, roots, walnuts and hazelnuts.

A VERITABLE BESTIARY.

In Lascaux, the other animals seldom served as food ; but large numbers of them can be seen on the cave walls and roof. All of them are, of course, wild animals ; none are domestic.

Horses predominate (they are four times more numerous than cattle or deer). Most of them are small horses, very similar to Prjwalski's horses who could still be found last century in the steppes of Mongolia where they were discovered in 1880. They lived in timorous herds led by a stallion. Nowadays, they have probably died out in the wild but large numbers of them can still be seen in zoos. They are a small breed (7 ft 4 ins to 9 ft 4 ins in length, ranging from 12 to just over 14 hands high) with a massive head on a thick neck.

24 — Axial Gallery. Between the Chinese horses and the Bulls' Chamber are three red cows, their heads forming a circle around a sketch of a small horse outlined in red on the roof of the gallery at its narrowest point. The body of one of the cows stretches from one wall of the cave to the other.

25 — Axial Gallery. *A view of the end of the gallery, looking towards the Bulls' Chamber. On the right is the great black bull (photo 26), a horse and a sign.*

The mane stands up like a brush and they have long, dark tails (3 ft to 3 ft 8 ins in length). They have a bay coat ranging in shade from reddish to yellow-brown, and their coats are longer and lighter-coloured in the winter. The backbone is emphasised by a brown line known as a «donkey stripe», while their withers bear one or more dark markings. Their legs are also darker, sometimes with brown stripes. They do not have the same number of chromosomes as today's horses. Other wild horses are the tarpins of the steppes or forests. Common for many years in Europe and fairly similar to the previous species (with a grey or mouse-grey coat), the breed died out over the last two centuries. Artificially-bred tarpans have been reared this century, using a cross between various tarpinoid horses such as the Konik. In the drawings in Lascaux (and therefore probably in the minds of the Early Magdalenians), cattle occupied second place, ranking equal with deer. Far behind the horses. The cattle in question are aurochs and bison.

The *aurochs*, or primitive ox, indicates the existence of a more temperature climate than would the bison. A few figures serve to underline the strength of this animal. It was almost 10 ft in length and stood nearly 6 ft high at the withers. It could weigh anything up to one tonne. Its horns could measure 32 ins in length (cows were 25 % smaller and lighter than bulls). Our domestic cattle descend from these impressive, aggressive ancestors which had a black-brown or reddish-brown coat with a lighter stripe along the backbone. The coat was long and curly in the winter and short in the summer. The head was massive, especially in bulls which had a white ring around the muzzle and chin, a curved forehead, and long white horns with a black tip. The belly and interior of the legs were light-coloured. The aurochs lived in small herds (one bull, a few cows and the calves). The last wild ox died Poland in 1627 but, between the wars, zoologists managed to breed neo-aurochs (which resembled the aurochs depicted on old engravings and paintings), by crossing various European breeds of cattle that were still in a very primitive stage of development. The numerous aurochs, which resembled the paintings in Lascaux, confirmed the success of this re-breeding experiment, but once a species has died out it can never fully be revived.

26 and 27 — Axial Gallery. The great reddish-black aurochs (L = over 10 ft), obviously a bull. The head is shown in profile with a C-shaped muzzle emphasised by the line of the lower lip, the horns are depicted from three-quarters angle. The dewlap is protruding. The front legs are thrown forwards and one hoof is shown from front view, with the two cloots clearly visible. Covered by the body of the

The other bovine present in Lascaux was the *bison*. The present European bison is its descendent and it, too, is very impressive with a length of between 10 and 11 ft, a height of 6 ft 6 ins at the withers, and a weight of up to one tonne. The chest is massive, and covered with long dark hair. The head hangs low and the forehead is vertical (like us). The bison has a tuft of hair at the top of its head and a beard. Its horns (which can reach a length of 20 ins) protrude sideways from the forehead and curve upwards then frontwards, the tips pointing inwards. The coat is very thick but rubs off in patches during the spring when the new coat begins to grow. Bison have a short tail (18 to 20 ins) with increasingly long

hair towards the tip but there is no final tuft and it looks rather ridiculous. The withers are raised because of the protruberance formed by spinal vertebrae and the cervico-dorsal line therefore bears four successive humps viz. the shaggy forehead, the tuft of fur between and in front of the horns, a mass of fat at the neck covered with fur, and the long high withers. Once an animal of the steppes, the European bison now lives in forests. But the present bison in the Bialowieza Forest in Poland are descended from domesticated bison (hence there is a rather worrying degree of in-breeding). Left in the wild, old bulls live in isolation, forming a separate herd. During the breeding season, the herd divides into

small groups (eight to ten animals), each led by the oldest cow.

A mediocre, and incomplete, engraving in the Apse at Lascaux seems to depict a *musk ox*, or ovibos. This large goat-like creature (6 ft to over 8 ft in length, with a height at the withers of 3 ft 8 ins to 4 ft 10 ins, and a weight of 4 to 6 cwt) is especially remarkable for its rough, fluffed out coat that hides its shape and makes the animal look bigger than its really is. The horns, too, are very unusual. The base of each horn widens out into a plate, sometimes forming a sort of half-helmet. The horn bends downwards very close to the cheek then suddenly bends upwards like a hook. Musk oxen now live in the frozen north, indeed they

bull are two smaller red cows and four horned heads of young cattle. In front of the muzzle is a branch-shaped sign and an unfinished painting of a blackish-brown horse. Between the two front legs is a small hole filled with clay. It bears the imprint of scaffolding timber.

were only discovered during the last century. They prefer very cold climates.

The Cervides painted or engraved on the walls of the cave in Lascaux are all (with one exception, a reindeer) *stags* or *does*, which indicates a period of climatic warming. They are common deers, similar to our European Elaphurus or red deers. They are 5ft 6 ins to 8 ft 10 ins in length, 2 ft 6 ins to 5 ft in height, and they weigh between 165 and 748 lbs. The head has a pointed muzzle and is held erect. Only the buck has antlers, which are cast every winter. The long spike has numerous tines pointing forwards and it ends in a fork or palm that varies greatly from one animal to another. As the stag ages, its «head» becomes increasingly well-armed. Apart from the autumn breeding period when it calls the females by troating before mounting them, a stag lives alone or, more often, in a mixed or all-male herd, a sort of «club» in which it spends the winter.

Ibex are now only to be found in high mountains on the edge of the snow line and are difficult to approach. But the situation was quite different in the days when Lascaux was inhabited. They lived in our regions but did not appreciate high temperatures. These goatlike creatures, which were still fairly large (ranging in length from almost 4 ft to 5 ft 8 ins, for a height of between 2 ft 2 ins and 3 ft 6 ins and a weight of between 77 lbs and 3 cwt) had very unusual horns. They were Alpine ibex; the horns are ringed and describe the arc of a circle towards the front. They can be up to almost 3 ft long on males. The animals have a sturdy body and a short, sometimes turned on before, tail. They have cloven hooves, which enable them to run fast and leap across rough ground. These ibex are best-suited to the natural parks in the Alps. During the winter breeding season, males and females mix, of course. During the remainder of the year, the males live in groups while the females form a separate herd with the kids. In summer, the males clash, often participating in long, ritualised fights which decide their hierarchical position within their herd. During the breeding season, the males avoid each other. The ibex of today are well-protected from their natural enemies (wolves, lynx, and bears).

The *felines* engraved in Lascaux, unlike the great herbivorous animals in the main galleries, are relegated to a modest side passage. In fact, they are few in number (less than ten) and their outline is drawn in very summary fashion without any great detail. They are probably lions without manes (or cave lions), which differ only very slightly from the lions of today (between 5 ft 8 ins and 6 ft 4 ins in length, with the males weighing between 3 and 6 1/2 cwt, and females from just over 2 to 3 1/2 cwt, each of them having a tuft of fur at the end of their 3 ft long tails). The mediocre drawings of them here perhaps give some indication of the cats' behaviour : prides with two or three males for between five and ten females, living discreetly and, partly at least, as nocturnal animals. Lions are animals of the steppe and although nowadays their natural habitat is Africa (where they can be found even on high slopes in Kenya) they were not originally from the tropics.

The bear hiding behind a large slash of paint representing an aurochs in the Bulls' Chamber is

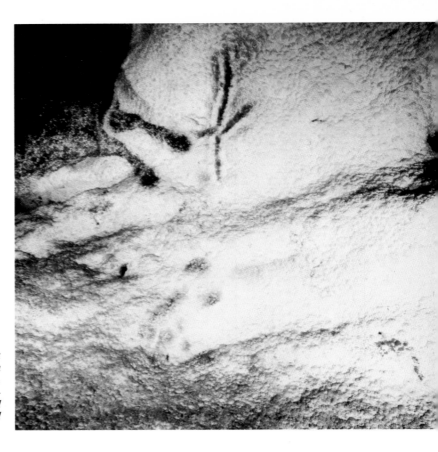

29 — Axial Gallery. Traces and black pigment beneath the branch-shaped sign in front of the reddish horse (photo 28). A. Glory believes the traces once represented the head of a feline turned towards the left (round ears, forehead and muzzle).

without doubt a *brown bear* (or perhaps a bear cub) and it is similar to the bears of today (ranging in length from 6 ft 6 ins to 9 ft 9 ins, and weighing between 3 and 15 cwt or more at the start of the winter). Everybody, one might say from childhood onwards, knows its brown fur, its head with the slightly rounded forehead (unlike the forehead of its ancestors, the cave bear), its dog-like muzzle, its round ears, its front and back paws with soft rubbery pads and long curved claws that cannot be retracted, and its occasional propensity to stand erect. It is known that bears, which are omnivorous creatures, need a very wide territory. It is a very shy animal which hibernates in caves in winter (this is where the cubs are born and where they live for some time) and leaves its claw marks on the clay or rock. Bears do not appear to have entered Lascaux and it would be very naive to imagine that there was ever a battle between Magdalenians and bears or lions for possession of the cave...

Apart from all the animals which we can still see today in their natural environment or in zoos, the rhinoceros depicted in Lascaux is extinct, a fossil in fact. It is a *woolly rhinoceros* from cold climates, with cellular nostrils (this feature was inexistent or only partially developed in its predecessors). This animal may have given rise to the legends about dragons. It disappeared from the planet thousands of years ago but much is known about it. Like the mammoths, numerous woolly rhinoceros have

(On previous pages)
28 — Axial Gallery. The reddish horse (L = 10 ft) outlined in black, which seems to be moving away towards the end of the gallery. The mane and beard are feathery, and the breast and neck are clearly stencilled in. The hindquarters and hind legs are somewhat clumsy. Again there is a branch-shaped symbol in front of the animal. Below is a rocky traverse that was used to wedge the joists of the scaffolding on which the Magdalenian painters worked.

been discovered with their hide, bone and fur intact, preserved by the ice in the far north of Siberia. It was as impressive an animal as the largest of today's African rhinoceros (9 ft 9 ins to 13 ft in length, nearly 5 ft tall at the withers, and with a weight that could reach 2 tonnes). The rather mis-shapen outline of the rhinoceros is familiar to everybody - a long narrow head held horizontally or bent low, large ears, bulging abdomen, short sturdy legs, stringy tail and, of course, the two keratinous horns (the one on the forehead resembles a rose thorn while the one on the nose can be almost 5 ft long). The unusual characteristic of the woolly rhinoceros was its thick coat consisting of thick black underfur and long straight overhair of a reddish black colour on its flanks. The fur was particularly thick around the neck and shoulders, which increased the height of the fatty hump on its withers. It is known that Siberian rhinoceros lived alone or in a family with females and offspring, either in the steppes or in the pinewoods where it fed off the pine branches or off the lower leaves of other trees. In winter, the animals lived off their reserves of fat. Nobody knows why the species died out (like its contemporary, the mammoth, which is not depicted in Lascaux).

Men

SETTING THE RECORD STRAIGHT.

Lascaux does not date from the mists of time, as is shown by a few figures, albeit rounded up or down.

Life (in the form of a tiny blue algae) appeared on our planet two billion years ago. As for dinosaurs, they are 200 million years old. The first man (*Homo habilis*, who made the earliest-known tools) lived in Africa 2 million years ago. Man has inhabited Périgord for 200,000 years or a little over.

The cave as Lascaux was discoverd by Cro-Magnon man 17,000 years ago. One might say, only 17,000...

PEOPLE LIKE YOU AND ME.

Cro-Magnon man looked like us physically and he had the same degree of intelligence (though he lacked our acquired cultural knowledge). Like us, he used language and was subject to tears and laughter. Like us, he had his good points and his bad. He lived an active life in a natural environment, and most of the population was young.

They were modern men and we are all Cro-Magnons. Truth to tell, our predecessor, Neanderthal Man, who lived not far away, in Le Moustier for example, was already well developed. In the language of anthropologists, he was already *sapiens* (knowledgeable). As for us, we are *Homo sapiens sapiens*, i.e. twice as knowledgeable. Or so they say.

Like us, Cro-Magnon man, in the days when Lascaux was inhabited, had an advanced civilisation and life was organised in a social culture. These men were nei ther brutes nor tramps. They lived in comfortable huts built in the open or beneath the entrances of rock shelters or caves. Gradually, they developed flint tools (blades, lamelers and scrapers, burins, piercers, etc.) and hunting weapons made of antlers (spearheads, spear straighteners, and pro-bably spearthrowers or even bows). They were not dressed in rags. The large number of needles (with eyes) found in their houses proves that they had an interest in sewing. They also had free time on their hands. A Magdalenian's day-to- day life included no more than a few hours of work, making tools, hunting, fishing etc.

These people lived the existence of semi-nomadic huntsmen, in families or groups of families. They had a base camp in the centre of the hunting territory and mobile camps near places through which reindeer had to pass (migration trails, fords, springs). They were meat-eaters, their diet being a combination of reindeer meat, fat and marrow varied by the inclusion of wild plants. Hunting (and fishing) were doubtless reserved for the male population, as they are in all civilisations ; the women were probably respon sible for gathering plants. This ensured perfect environmental equilibrium.

(Overleaf)
30 — Axial Gallery. The «leaping» cow (L = 5 ft. 6 ins) facing the great black bull, a picture that is unusually full of movement. The hind legs are raised in a position that in anatomically incorrect and the tail is curved like a whip. In front of the cow is a quadrangle ; below are numerous small horses.

31 — Axial Gallery. Below the «leaping» cow are the famous «ponies». These five small horses are depicted trotting in a line on an imaginary stretch of ground (formed by the ledge of the rock) towards the entrance to the cave. The tail of one of them is shown between the raised hooves of the cow and the head of another horse. The combination of large cow and small horses is frequent in Lascaux.

32 — Axial Gallery. One of the «ponies» (photo 31). Its outline lacks detail. The mane is raised, its tail is thick and long. In the rougher parts of the painted area are small crystals of calcite.

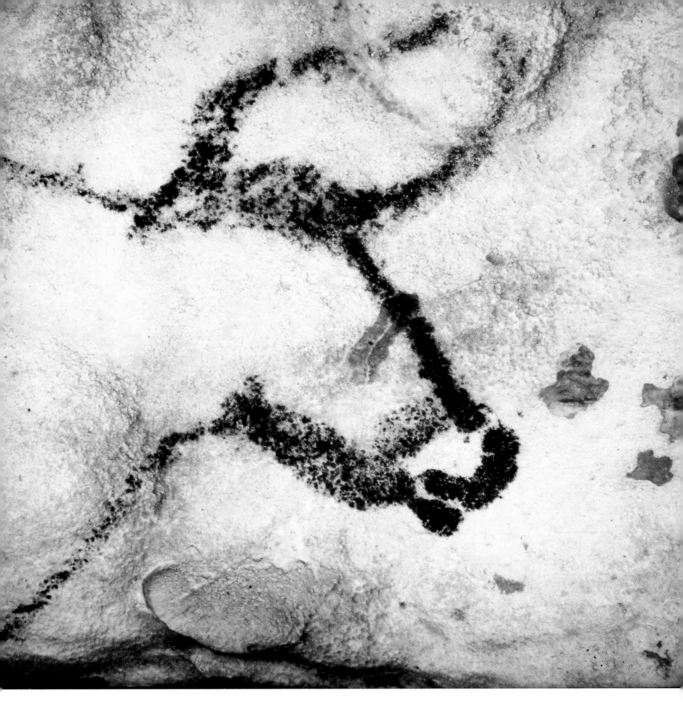

33 — Axial Gallery. *Above the leaping cow on the roof of the gallery is the head of a large black bull which closely resembles the ones in the Bulls' Chamber (photos 2, 4, 5, 9, and 11). Note the irregular way in which the pigment has been applied to the calcite crystals on the wall of rock.*

38

All advanced technology (and the techniques used in the Upper Paleolithic are exactly that) is accompanied by a transmission of technical information, and the method used to cut flint or antlers spread throughout Europe. Neither are beliefs and religious rites (graves, and decora ted caves) limited to this area. As you know, Man is a religious animal.

Magdalenians had no villages and problems relating to the population explosion were unknown ; nor did they have crops or herds. Life expectancy was short, but there has been no proof of murders, war, or cannibalism at that time.

A LONG APPRENTICESHIP.

It was Cro-Magnon man who invented the art of drawing, on the banks of the Vézère, some 30,000 years ago. It was here that one or more men first had the idea of tracing out on a flat surface of the rock a two-dimensional representation of what they saw in nature. They moved on to draw in relief and in three dimensions. They drew animals (many of which remained unfinished) and women's and men's genitals. And most of these early works from the Aurignacian are vigorous engravings on blocks of limestone or on the walls of rock shelters that have since caved in.

Gradually, during the Gravettian Period (approximately 20,000 to 25,000 years ago), these early artists took their courage in both hands and decorated the walls of a few small, shallow caves and of the rock shelters in which they lived (Laussel, Oreille d'Enfer, Poisson rock shelters near Les Eyzies, or Pair-non-Pair cave in Gironde). Their style had evolved. The outlines of animals were less gauche, and increasingly detailed. The third dimension began to make its appearance, and there was an attempt at perspective and a representation of volume. In the Solutrean Period (approximately 18,000 years ago, or one thousand years before Lascaux), great artists carved wonderful bas-reliefs of animals in a style that was a precursor of Lascaux

(Pataud museum and Le Fourneau du Diable in Dordogne, Roc de Sers in Charente).

THE PAINTERS
AND ENGRAVERS
OF LASCAUX.

Lascaux came into existence at the end of this long period of apprenticeship. The period between the invention of drawing (30,000 to 35,000 years ago) and Lascaux (17,000 years ago) was as long as the period separating us from the civilisation of Lascaux.

And in the light of tallow lamps, this cave appeared as the first of the deep cave-sanctuaries. The decoration of this cave is fairly stereotyped and the same layout will be found, with numerous variations (as is the case in our churches) throughout the Magdalenian Period. In most cases, horses and cattle were represented on the main panels, surrounded by other species. The drawings of men (which are rare and very simplified) and pictures of fierce animals (e.g. big cats or bears) are often relegated to the ends of galleries. Geometric symbols are commonplace everywhere.

Lascaux is the oldest of the deep, decorated caves, as well as being the most unusual. During the remainder of the Magdalenian, there were to be many other decorated caves (over a hundred in all) in France and Spain, many of them very attractive but much more traditional in style (Font de Gaume, les Combarelles, Rouffignac in Dordogne, Niaux in Ariège, Altamira in Spain, etc.). It was during this period that the art of making decorative objects or furnishings developed. Lascaux, then, seems to have been a trial run during the early days of the Magdalenian, and it turned out to be a masterpiece. Rather like a fireworks display beginning with the finale.

The painters and engravers were craftsmen, very probably released from the burden of their daily work by other members of the group. Professionals, as Prof. André Leroi-

Gourhan liked to say to us. Nothing is known of their living quarters but much is known about their art, their techniques, and their everyday life.

It is obvious that they patiently acquired great gestual mastery for the sureness of the painted or engraved lines was not the result of improvisation. Drawing errors, the so-called «second thoughts», or errors in proportion are few and far between. These craftsmen had acquired real painting techniques (lightly or strongly coloured lines and flat tints), they knew how to use stencils, and how to engrave, chiselling into the rock. They invented engraving-painting-engraving (a three-stage process consisting of an engraved sketch, the painting of the subject matter, and the outline and details engraved against this background). They knew how to frame the outlines of animals and make them appear to move across the rough surface of the rock face by implicitly suggesting the ground, playing with proportions, and carefully positioning the animals whose outlines appear close together, adjacent, touching, cutting across each other or more or less merging into each another.

Yet the artists remained hunters who knew every detail of the animals' anatomy (e.g. the antlers of the deer, or the coat of the aurochs), their reactions (ibex fighting, the «clubs» of old stags or male ibex) and a few more precise details (the winter coat of certain horses, the sloughing of the bison's fur, and the back-to-back attitude of bison).

These observations of animal life are not transcribed by the artists with a slavish will to depict reality. The outlines are reproduced with very unusual deformities (artistic devices, specific techniques and graphic guidelines) that these men had only just invented and which they systematically applied to all their drawings. It is well-known that Renoir did not paint women in the same way as Bernard Buffet, and that Giacometti's statues are very different to the ones produced by Maillol.

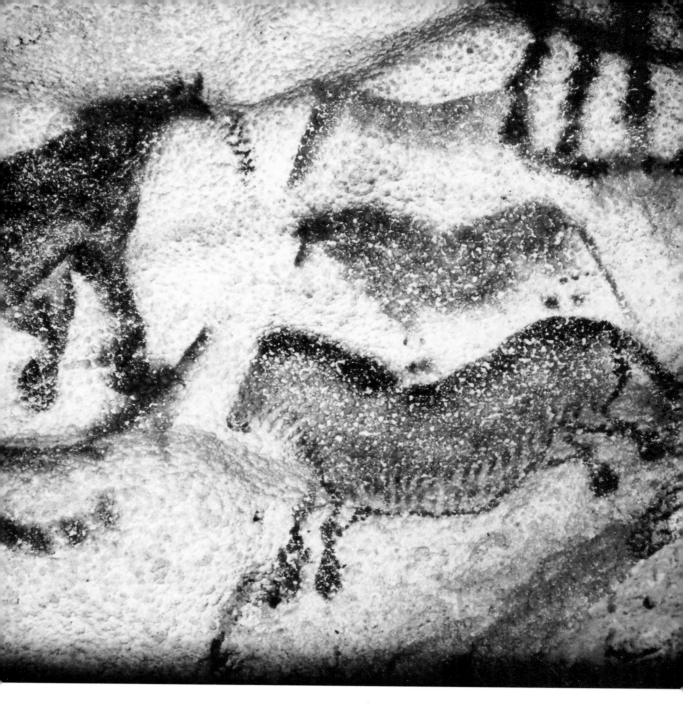

34 — Axial Gallery. *The leaping cow is surrounded by horses, some finished, others incomplete. Some of the horses' coats are very detailed, and spotted with calcite crystals. They also have longer hair under their bellies, striped manes and shoulder markings.*

(Overleaf)
35 — Axial Gallery. *Ibex fighting. One of them is drawn in black, the other (with the markings on the belly) consists of lines of yellow dots. They are male Alpine ibex with long horns one above the other, and short beard and tail. Between them is another rectangular symbol ; above them are the last of the horses round the leaping cow.*

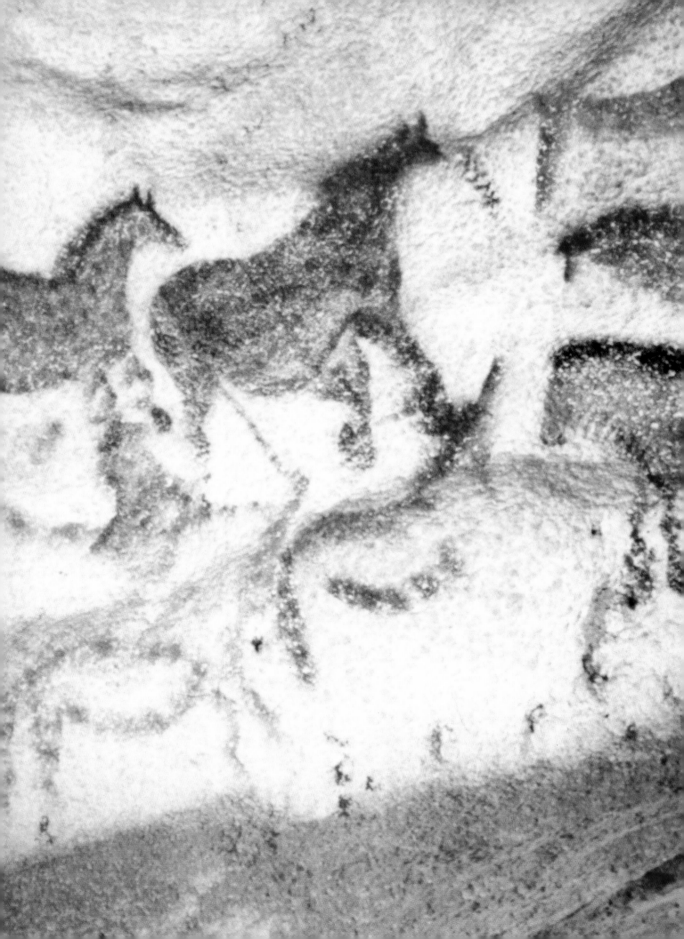

The animals are carefully positioned to suit the appearance of the cave itself and the previous layout of the underground passages. There is a circular painted frieze in the Bulls' Chamber with the right and left halves in opposition ; there is a series of decorations in the corridor in the Axial Gallery but with a number of red cows extending up on the ceiling forming a sort of rose window, and a «falling» horse at the end of the gallery. The Passage and Apse have small engravings, apparently scattered at random, in palimpsests that were probably always difficult to make out ; the Nave has engravings, paintings-engravings and paintings, some in lines, others not. The Pit contains drawings outlined in black (the man and bison scene) and there are engravings which are intermingled to varying extents in the narrow Felines Gallery.

In other words, this is a cave over 270 yds. long decorated with a majestic set of paintings (near the cave mouth), a miscellany of engravings (in an adjacent gallery), more engravings and/or paintings forming friezes (slightly further into the cave) and two strange smaller galleries, one of them painted, the other engraved and painted.

On the walls of rock, the animals rub shoulders with each other or merge totally or partially into each other, with no respect for the relative sizes of the different species and with no obvious connection between them except in the very few character studies : bisons shown back to back, ibex fighting, stag and ibex «clubs». Rather like words picked out of a dictionary without any obvious syntax or punctuation. The only narrative scene is the one at the bottom of the Pit. A man is stretched out on the ground opposite a bison that is also injured (the scene includes other detailed features). It is an unexpected composition in this deserted spot

Likewise the animals in Lascaux are not photographs of living models. The horses, aurochs, bison, and stags are pot-bellied (even the males) ; they have sturdy legs depicted in movement and hooves painted as if seen from above (i.e. round or oval, some cloven, others not). The heads are sometimes small and elongated. The fur is suggested by a pigmented flat tint and in some cases is set out geometrically.

Perspective is carefully twisted. The head and body of the animals are shown in profile but the horns and chest of the cattle are seen from a three-quarter angle. The stags' antlers (and the horns of the ibex) are shown as being almost vertical, one drawn above the other, sloping towards the back.

Lascaux is the eye of the hunter and the hand of the artist. This is doubtless why this cave occupies such a special place in the history of prehistoric art. In fact, before Lascaux, ornamentation was not bad at all ; after Lascaux, it is very well done. But in Lascaux itself, it is beautiful.

RELIGIOUS ART IN A CAVE-SANCTUARY.

The whole mythological background of the Magdalenian Period is present here with its heroes viz. the fundamental dichotomy (horses and cattle), the hierarchy of other animals, man and geometric symbols. Yet there is also much, much more.

Almost at every step, one is faced with the leitmotiv of the cave i.e. a group consisting of one large bovine and several small horses, reminding visitors that Lascaux is not just another art exhibition held somewhere in the provinces.

*37 — **Axial Gallery.** The end of the gallery consists of a sort of pillar of rock skirted on the right by the final twist in the passageway. The reddish horse (photo 28) and the black ibex (photo 36) flank the pillar sporting the famous «falling» horse. The roof forms a natural channel.*

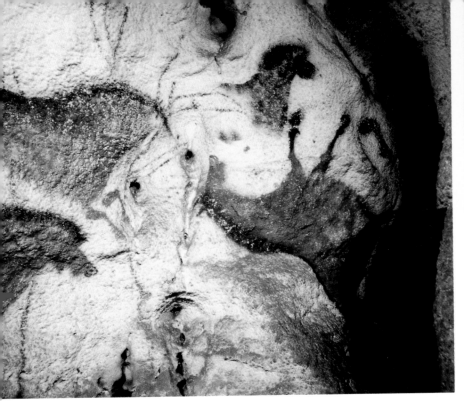

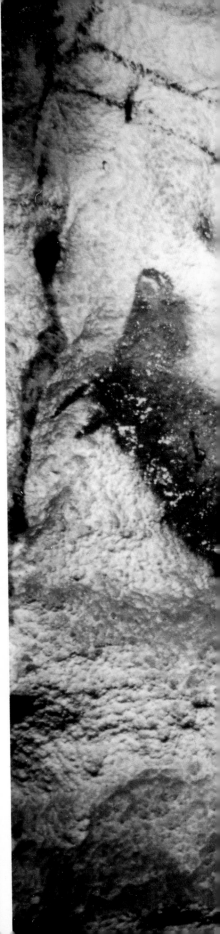

38 — Axial Gallery. *The «falling» horse (L = approx. 6 ft. 6 ins) is depicted taking a tumble. The ears turned down towards the back show fear and aggressivity. The hindquarters, which are represented perfectly although in a different plane, are not visible here. Around the animal are three horses and two large branch-shaped symbols.*

39 — Axial Gallery. *These two horses face the «falling» horse. The top one, with the thin head and no hind legs nor belly, has raised its front legs out of the way of its companion's head. The bottom horse is complete and shows the usual graphic treatment of the horse in Lascaux. Beneath its hooves is a row of dots.*

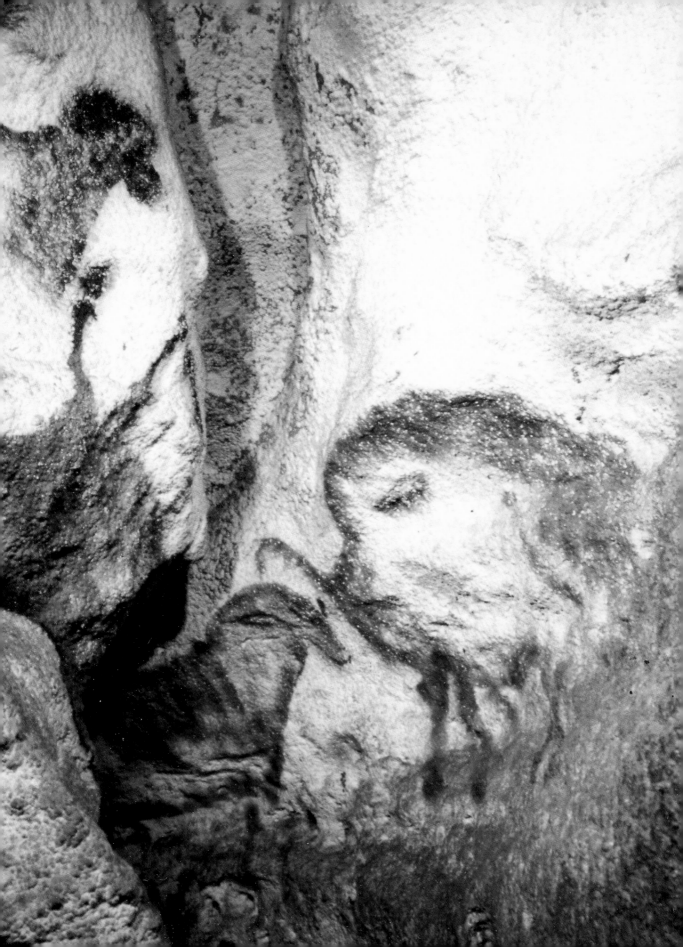

41 — Axial Gallery. *The second last horse in the final turn of the passageway. It has a striped coat. Its head is drawn beneath the raised tail of the bison.*

The numerous, complex, and varied signs or symbols add still further to this strange atmosphere. They can be seen everywhere and can be grouped into three main categories i.e. full signs (rectangles, ovals, etc.), probably representing feminine symbols, thin signs (sticks with or without lateral development) which probably have masculine overtones, and punctuations about which nothing is known. Some of the signs are particular to Lascaux and the few caves from the same period (rectangles in Lascaux, Gabillou and Villars) and resemble ethnic markers. Other signs, which are few in number here, are more common in Ariège or Spain (signs in the shape of a club, called «claviforms»). Yet the meaning of all these signs remains a mystery, even though there is an instinctive feeling that, in Lascaux, as A. Leroi-Gourhan said to us, man «came very close to writing». After all, would one of our present-day signs (for example a heart pierced by an arrow, a simple cross, or the «No Entry» roadsign) be intelligible to a creature from outer space or even to one of the last «primitive peoples» of our planet ?

There are other strange elements, though, in Lascaux. The animals depicted here (horses, aurochs, bison, stags, does, ibex, bears, and rhinoceros) were not hunted or eaten by Magdalenian people, as shown by the scraps of bone found in the ground. Their main prey was the reindeer. And on the walls of rock, among the 600 paintings and 1,500 engravings in the cave, only one represents a reindeer - and even that is open to question. A sad thought for those who believed that cave art was a magic art form, that a guarantee of a successful hunt required no more than a few outlines of animals on a wall of rock before which the people could cut a few dance figures to the sound of bone pipes. It was not that simple...

And in addition to all that we can see in the cave, there is all that remained unsaid and unrepresented. In

(On previous pages)
40 — Axial Gallery. *In the narrow turn at the end of the gallery opposite the falling horse is a red bison with an enormous hump and a raised tail, followed by two horses.*

42 — Axial Gallery. The last horse in the final turn of the passageway. Its clumsy outline follows the steeply-sloping roof of the gallery.

Lascaux, as in the other decorated caves, there is no attempt to depict the ground, landscape, plants, trees or rocks and there are no objects (except perhaps a sling and a spear in the scene in the Well). Nor are there any small animals. And with two exceptions, the few animals which seem to have been wounded by spears do not seem to be in pain.

Lascaux, a place of worship, was undoubtedly very popular. This is shown by the numerous objects left behind (e.g. more than a hundred lamps), the way in which the ground has been trodden down, and the traces of usage on the walls (rubbings, lines that are not always as expected). The artists made themselves comfortable before beginning their work. They had poles to climb up or

sophisticated scaffolding (traces of this have been discovered), and the ground was covered with grasses and artemisia in the Passage, where they had to sit down to be able to paint.

All these elements show that Art in Lascaux was designed to serve a veritable religious cult, which was organised and collective ; it had no connection with any magical rites which are always more or less marginal and short-lived, as well as being individual. People have also wrongfully spoken of witchcraft, the black magic which calls on the spirits of Evil («it is so useful for some to look, in words that are devoid of any precise meaning, for precisions that the figures do not provide», said A. Leroi-Gourhan).

Lascaux is much more like a cathedral, with its nave and side aisles, than the smoke-filled lair of a magician or wizard. Yet religious motives do not preclude aesthetic preoccupations (or even ulterior motives related to some form of magic), as we can see from the art and architecture of our Gothic cathedrals.

Lascaux, by its complexity, and its graphic, symbolic and archaeological uniformity, is now considered to have been the work of a few professionals of the Faith, belonging to one or more Magdalenian families over one or more generation.

48

A THEATRE IN DARKNESS.

When the cave was first discovered in 1940 and again during excavations to install ventilation shafts, numerous objects were found and collected. Strangely enough, Lascaux has never been subjected to a veritable archaeological dig (with one exception, in the Well, and its scope was very limited) and the ground was disturbed during preparations prior to its opening to the public. The objects left behind by the Magdalenians form an extraordinary set of bric-a-brac, now scattered among numerous collections. Yet they have all been studied thanks to the persistance of Arlette Leroi-Gourhan and her team, and they have made it possible to reconstitute the life of the artists as well as of the prehistoric visitors to Lascaux.

The cave was never a home but, as people passed through it or stayed there for limited periods, numerous objects were dropped on the ground or left behind on the shelves in the rock and, more particularly on the ground where sediments gradually covered them up. The ensuing archaeological layer is quite unique, for it has none of the successive levels observed in shelters that were lived in for long periods of time. The layer is uniform and just below the surface of the ground, protected by a few inches of sand, clay or calcite. The cave itself was sealed up shortly after its use by the Early Magdalenians when the roof in the entrance collapsed.

The objects are known to have belonged to the artists themselves, for two reason. Firstly, the layer also contains the tools and ingredients that they used (the engravers' flints with corners rounded off by rubbing against the rock, pigments in the form of pencils or powders, pallets, crushers). And secondly, some of the objects in this layer are decorated with symbols that are specific to the art seen on the walls in Lascaux (double herringbones fitted one into the other on a sandstone lamp and a spearhead, or a star with six rays centering on a dot on a spear).

Their technical appearance shows that the flints are indeed the ones used during the Early Magdalenian Period, as are the austerely decorated spears.

And in the same layer beneath the ground, the pollens (and timber residues) correspond to the period of climatic warming (the intermediate period of Lascaux) that is also evident in other sites, while the charcoal can be dated precisely to 15,000 B.C. by means of carbon-dating techniques.

*43 — **The Passage.** Finely-engraved horses on the roof of the gallery. They are all drawn in the same style but their attitudes vary (legs drawn up, sometimes in an abnormal fashion, heads bent down etc.). Some of the animals have excessively long tails (survey by A. Glory).*

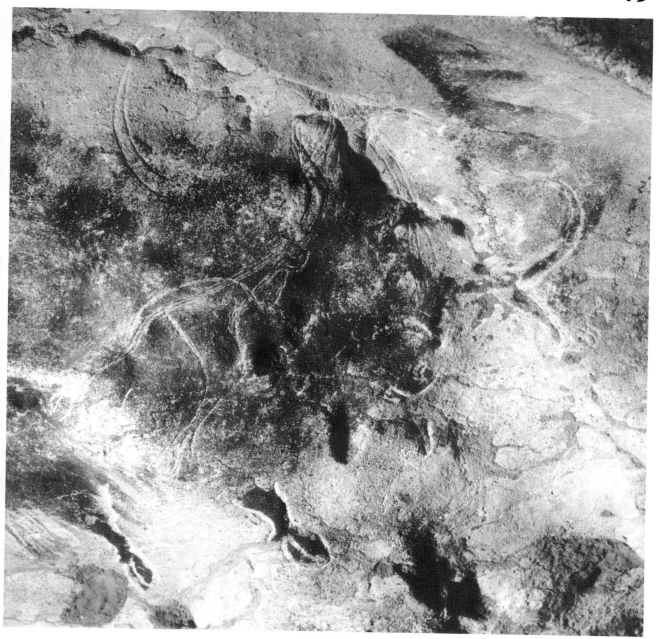

*44 — **The Imprint Panel (Nave).** Three interlinked bison. The forequarters of the first two, facing to the right, are slightly out of line with each other. The heads are carefully engraved in great detail with the eyes, nostrils, beards and lyre-shaped horns (as if seen from the front) Cutting across the second bison head is the engraving of the hindquarters of a third animal. The outline of the hind leg can be seen quite clearly. Note the cloven oval hooves.*

FLASH BACK.

Let us try to imagine exactly what occurred in Lascaux.

The tallow lamps project a *flickering light* on the walls of rock but it is sufficient to enable men to move around and work. The air smells slightly of burnt fat. One of the lamps looks like a thick, but highly-polished spoon shaped out of a piece of red sandstone from what is now Corrèze (where the tiny village of Collonges-la-Rouge, or Collonges the Red, is well-known). Another lamp is no more than a small block of local limestone carefully hollowed out using a flint pick. These lamps worked in a closed circuit rather like old-fashioned oil lamps with a fibre wick soaking in the melted fat.

45 and 46 — The Black Cow Panel (Nave). *This large reddish black cow (L = 6 ft. 8 ins) whose shape is emphasised by an engraved line dominates a whole row of small horses which are also painted and engraved or only engraved. The pictorial representation of the cow is typical of the art work in Lascaux but there are a few specific details i.e. the*

47 — The Black Cow Panel (Nave). *Two painted and engraved horses facing each other. They have striped manes, and their ears are set on the top of their heads (close-up of photo 45).*

black-tipped horns, the small line in front of the muzzle (perhaps the cow's breath ?), the protruding hindquarters, the short, slender legs with narrow, elongated cloven hooves (similar to the ones on the stags), and the double line along the belly. The horses on the left have oval hooves ; the ones on the right are round.

48 — The Black Cow Panel (Nave). The hind legs of the black cow rest on two large partitioned rectangles (so-called «coats-of-arms») painted in a «patchwork» design. The outline is engraved. The panel shows a three-stage technique which is common in this gallery - an engraved sketch, a colour wash, and engraved lines emphasising the general shape and most important details. On the left is another partitioned rectangle (close-up of photos 45 and 46).

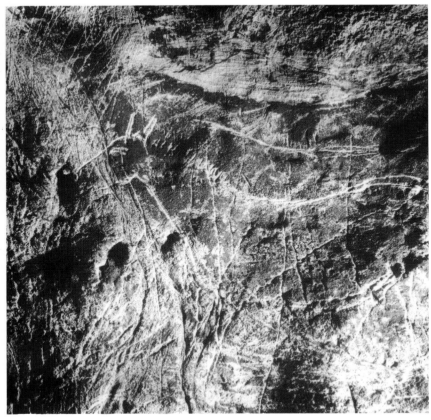

*49 and 50 — The Black Cow Panel
(Nave). In the middle of the engraved
lines, on the shoulder of one of the large
horses, is the outline of a small horse
(this is perhaps a mare and its foal). The
mare's hindquarters are meticulously
painted and engraved. The hind legs have
oval hooves with a spur above. The left
leg is separated from the belly by a white
area, a similar technique to the one use
in other paintings (e.g. photos 3, 22, 23,
and 28). The mare is followed by two
other horses, also painted and engraved,
one above the other (close-up of
photo 45).*

Most of the other lamps (more
than one hundred of them in all) are
plain slabs of limestone no bigger
than the palm of one or two hands.
They are naturally flat or very
slightly hollow and have not been res-
haped. The scorch marks on them (a
reddened and blackened area) and
experiments have shown that they
worked in an open circuit like a
candle. A piece of tallow was used as
fuel and a small bunch of fast-
burning twigs became the wick
impregnated with the melted fat. This
self-supporting system gives approximately as much light as a modern
candle (the flame melts the tallow
and produces grease which impre-
gnates the wick). Juniper was used as
a wick, as has been proved by the
analysis of sooty particles removed
from the lamps.

The art of engraving meant cutting
into the coarse, sandy wall of rock
with a sharp flint. The resultant line
is fine, with a triangular cross-section
which has now more or less worn
smooth. The artists did not use tools
for this work ; they engraved with

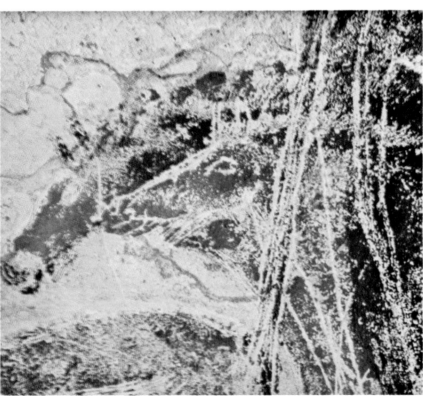

*51 — The Black Cow Panel (Nave). Two
horses' heads, painted and engraved one
behind the other, emerge from the rump
of the black cow. Their engraved outline
is partly included within the body of the
cow (close-up of photo 45).*

blades, mere flakes of flint. A few of these flints (27 out of 403) still bear traces of wear at one or more corners. This would be compatible with rubbing the blade across the sandstone limestone rock. The tools (end scrapers, burins, and piercers) bear no such traces, with the exception of one burin. Some of the blades consist of small isoceles triangles ; others were hafted and still bear traces of the binding agent, probably a mixture of resin and clay. Nobody knows what these blades were used for in Lascaux.

(Overleaf)

*52 — **The Stag Panel (Nave).** Four old stags' heads (Ht of each = over 3 ft), drawn in black lines using manganese. Behind them is a fifth head drawn in clay. They constitute a frieze over 16 ft. long. As in the Bulls' Chamber, one ear is set in the nape of the neck but in this instance the other ear is rather strangely set in the side of the neck. The large antlers are drawn as elsewhere in Lascaux (one more or less vertical and the other sloping towards the back). The tear bag beneath the eye has not been forgotten. The heads are all depicted in different attitudes. It has been thought that the herd is shown crossing a ford in a stream.*

53 — The back-to-back bisons (Nave). *All the usual stylistic features and perspectives found elsewhere in Lascaux are present in these two bull bisons with raised tails i.e. massive bodies, short legs depicted in movement, hooves seen from the front, highlighting of the background by means of strips left without pigment (legs, hindquarters). One of the bisons is casting his coat as is usual in the spring. The animals can be seen acting in this way in the natural environment.*

54 — The Apse. *The head of a stag (Ht = approx. 14 ins) with large antlers (one facing forwards, the other to the back). As in the stags painted in the Nave, one ear is set in the nape of the neck while the other is low down on the neck. The engraved line cuts into a rock with natural colouring and is clearly visible. All round the stag is a tangle of engraved figures that are much more difficult to decipher.*

The painters extracted the *pigments* from the cave floor or from places nearby. A large quantity of coloured powders and several dozen small blocks of pigment have been found. Scratches show that these blocks were used like «wax crayons» or were scraped to produce ochre powder. Iron oxides supplied the red (haematite) in hues ranging from reddish yellow to dark reddish brown, and the yellows (goethite and clay from the cave) ranging from pale yellow to a strong brown. Manganese dioxide, black iron oxide and charcoal provided the black pigments, with hues varying from olive grey to deep black. Crushed calcite produced a white powder. All these minerals were mixed with several parts of sand or clay, crushed in a mortar and bound with water from the cave. They were applied to the rock with fingers, a brush made of vegetable fibre or animal hair, or tufts of fur. The blowing of powder either straight from the mouth or through a bone pipe (a method that was often described to tourists by guides in the cave) was probably not a very common practice.

With their flickering lamps and all their equipment, the artists came face to face with the wall of rock. Most of the works of art in Lascaux are fairly high up, voluntarily spreading halfway onto the roof, out of reach. A veritable false floor was installed in the Axial Gallery, raising the ground level. We have found traces of the floor (holes into which the craftsmen slotted the beams or little ledges of rock) in the walls. In other galleries (e.g. the Bulls' Chamber, the Nave), the artists must have used roughly-lopped tree trunks, or they may have clambered up the walls of rock, using the natural footholds and handholds. These various types of *scaffolding* were certainly comfortable and well-built. They were made of oak, as shown by the tiny fragments that were examined under a microscope. In experiments, it has been proved feasible to cut scaffold-poles 4 inches thick using flint tools. The remains of a length of cord were discovered near one of the small swallow-holes in the cave.

Nobody knows exactly how the Magdalenians were dressed but some of the objects they wore have been found. There was *jewellery* made of fossils and shells, sometimes with a slit sawn in it so that it could be worn on a thong. There is a veritable collection of prehistoric jewellery with some fifteen shells originating in the local limestone or from fossil sites in the south-west, or from the beaches of the Atlantic and Mediterranean coasts where they were collected and brought back to Lascaux, probably in stages, after being passed from tribe to tribe. This taste for jewellery is not new ; it existed in the days of Neanderthal man. Yet the unexpected feature in this case is one fake shell, a small ovoid stone engraved with scratches that imitate natural twirls. A precursor of our costume jewellery, in fact.

A prolonged stay in the cave meant that the artists had to eat, and animal bones and the remains of these meals have been found in the archaeological site of the Nave and Axial Gallery which were, in some ways, *picnic areas*. Nine times out of ten, the remains are reindeer bones ; very occasionally, there are bones from roe deer, wild boar or hare. Only one or two traces of horse or red deer have been uncovered. No beef. The reindeers were young animals (between one and three years old), slaughtered early in the winter when the herd, which had spent the summer months on the slopes of the Massif Central, returned to the banks of the Vézère.

And that's it. For the moment, that's all there is to know, and modern prehistorians refuse to let their imagination run riot. In particular, nobody knows why so many spearheads have been found throughout Lascaux. They were all broken and decorated simply, with engravings of a double interlocked herring bone pattern, a star with six rays, an elongated saltire cross, or a plain horizontal line. In these grooves (as in the swirls of one shell) there are still a few traces of red pigment, either from the powders used by the artists or perhaps from the red ochre that tanned hides or coloured the skin of the indigenous people.

The objects found in Lascaux, then, give a clear picture of the work of the painters and engravers (most of the other decorated caves do not contain any such indications). Thanks to these remains, the cave paintings can be situated in time, with their graphic style and specific geometric symbols. The style is highly unusual, and was unknown to prehistorians prior to 1940, for other archaeological sites had not provided any comparable decorated artefact. And the small number of decorated caves, that were probably contemporary with Lascaux (Gabillou, Villars and the cave mouth at Saint-Cirq), were discovered later.

FOUR YOUTHS, SCIENTISTS, AND MODERN TECHNIQUES.

The story of the miraculous discovery of Lascaux has been told over and over again. The marvel was revealed thanks to the obstinacy of

(Overleaf)
55 — The drawings in the Pit (total length = 8 ft. 2 ins) cover one wall in the deepest corner of the cave. The exceptional feature of the drawing is its narrative character. A bison, its belly ripped open by a spear and with its entrails hanging out, is charging a man lying on the ground (a rudimentary outline of a figure with a bird's head, hands with four fingers, and an erect penis). The representation of the bison is very stiff but a sense of movement is given by two details i.e. the artificial angle of the head and the tail in the form of a whip. Beneath the drawings are two barbed signs. One of them, which may be a spearthrower, is topped by a remarkable drawing of a bird. To the left of the man is a double series of punctuation marks and a woolly rhinoceros that has no obvious connection with the scene as a whole.

56 — *The Pit.* *The woolly rhinoceros (close-up of photo 55) drawn in a thick black line. The front leg, dewlap and line of the belly with its overhair are all sketched in lightly. The drawing is very detailed. It shows the two horns, an ear on the forehead, a small eye and a raised tail. The back legs are depicted in perspective thanks to an area left unpainted. Below the tail is a six-pointed sign (the same sign, but in red, can be seen at the end of the Felines' Gallery).*

57 — *The Pit.* *An unfinished painting of a horse. The outline lacks precision but is similar to the ones of the painted and engraved horses in other parts of the cave. It stands opposite the scene depicting the man and the bison (photo 55).*

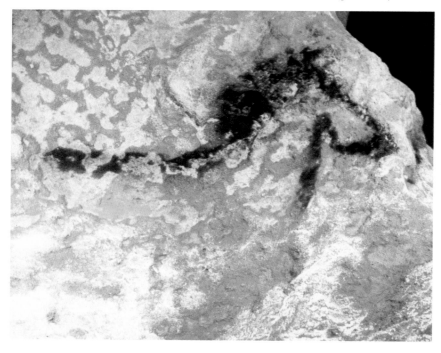

a young man from Montignac named Marcel Ravidat, then aged 17. On 8th September 1940, with a few friends and a dog, he discovered subsidence on the hillside above Montignac ; it had been caused by the uprooting of a large tree. A few days later, on Thursday 12th September, he returned to the spot with an oil lamp and a large knife, both of them homemade, in order to clear the entrance and slither down a cone of rubble. That day, he was accompanied by three other boys (Georges Agnel, Simon Coencas and Jacques Marsal). He tumbled into the cave and found his footing, quickly followed by the remainder of the group, in what we now know as the Bulls' Chamber. It was some twenty yards further on, in the Axial Gallery, that, by the smoky light of the oil lamp, the young explorers found the first paintings. They then went from one discovery to another and on the following day, Friday 13th, Marcel Ravidat let himself down a rope into the small pothole 16 ft. deep known as the Pit.

58 — *A pink sandstone lamp. (L = 9 ins), carefully gouged out to form a sort of spoon shape. It worked in an closed circuit like an oil lamp. The wick has left sooty deposits and has been proved to consist of juniper. The double interlocked chevrons engraved on the handle are similar to the ones on the walls of the cave.*

The boys' old primary teacher, Léon Laval, was told of their find a few days later. A few days after that saw the arrival of Father Henri Breuil, then considered as the «Pope» of Prehistory, followed by numerous prehistorians and a crowd of visitors. Despite the crowds, no damage was done thanks to careful supervision on the part of the four young men, and most of the easily-accessible artefacts were collected and put away in a safe place.

The earliest descriptions of the mural art were given by F. Windels and A.Laming-Emperaire, then by Father H. Breuil. They dealt mainly with the paintings. A. Leroi-Gourhan then published a few pages describing this sanctuary-cave.

Yet it was not until nearly forty years after the initial discovery in 1940 that the meticulous graphic surveys made of the engravings by Father A. Glory were published (1,500 graphics and more than 370 ft.

of tracing), with a commentary by D. Vialou. Also published were the results of the scientific research carried out by a team of specialists from several different disciplines, all of us working under the leadership of Arlette Leroi-Gourhan. The research dealt with the geology of the cave, its stratigraphics, analyses of sediments (radiocarbon, wood, pollens), remains of flint and bone, lamps, shells, animals, colouring agents, and access to the various walls of rock, in fact a veritable scientific analysis of the cave.

THE PATHS TO GLORY.

Lascaux was a sealed cave sloping downwards and ventilated by slow-moving draughts ; in 1940, it was suddenly and brutally brought into contact with the air outside. Visits to the cave by tourists from 1948 onwards took more than one million people through it in just over fifteen years. It was thought that every precaution had been taken to ensure that

the crowds would not alter or damage the works of art. A few drops of coloured water which dripped from the roof of the Axial Gallery in 1955 led to the installation, using a pneumatic drill, of the ducts for a heavy-duty ventilation and airing system in 1958. Yet occasionally, the treatment is worse than the disease and Lascaux was about to be put through the grist, as they say. It was at about this time that Mr. Ravidat noticed the first signs of the «green discase» caused by creeping plant growth that gradually spread in the warm, damp air beneath a lighting system that was almost permanently switched on.

The cave had to be closed to the public in 1963 and be decontaminated, a process that proved to be easy and did not cause any damage. It involved spraying the cave with a solution of antibiotics and formol. It was then that a new disease was diagnosed, «white discase». Calcite crystals showed a tendency to proli-

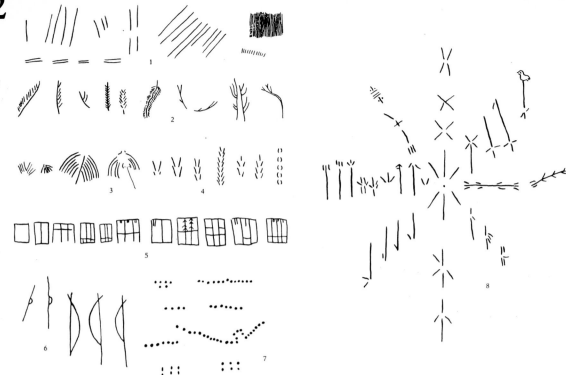

59 — This diagram summarizes the various types of signs discovered in Lascaux (a total of 400). 1, single or multiple stick drawn in parallel lines ; 2, branch-shaped signs ; 3, fan-shaped or «hut-shaped» signs ; 4, interlocked signs ; 5, quadrangles 6, club-shaped signs ; 7, punctuation marks grouped in various ways ; 8, signs that are apparently derived from star-shaped signs (the star is in the centre on this drawing) (after a. Leroi-Gourhan).

ferate because of the raised temperature, the humidity and the carbon dioxide produced by guided tours. There were few, or no, alterations visible to the naked eye but in the long run there was a high risk that the calcite would completely cover the paintings.

The cave was isolated from the outside world and, after long costly research, a simple remedy was installed - the cave was cooled down by a cold spot near the entrance (this re-established the original draughts along the Bulls' Chamber/Axial Gallery, thereby concentrating condensation on this spot rather than on the walls of the cave). The naturally-produced carbon dioxide was collected and evacuated, as were any seepages of water. Maintaining the parameters at a constant level (temperature, humidity and CO_2 of the air) meant that visits had to be restricted to five people per day. These measures are thought to be sufficient to preserve the decoration in the cave.

The closure of Lascaux to tourists explains the success of the reproductions of the painted galleries. In 1980, the Bulls' Chamber was reconstituted by photographic techniques (life-sized colour photos were transferred onto a base made to resemble the original chamber). This exhibition can now be seen in the Musée des Antiquités nationales in Saint-Germain-en-Laye. In 1983, another reproduction was completed on the spot near the original cave - it was called Lascaux II. In an enormous concrete bunker, there is an cement tunnel that reproduces every detail of the walls in the Bulls' Chamber and Axial Gallery. On this background, painters have reproduced the figures and symbols as exactly as possible, using the same materials as the Magdalenians. The air-conditioned exhibition also includes a small museum where we described the archaeological and historical environment of Lascaux, the elements used to date the finds, and the main graphic and stylistic

data, all of it designed to give a closer understanding of Lascaux. A few miles away, in Le Thot, is the Centre for the discovery of prehistoric art, which shows visitors the stages in the construction of Lascaux II and includes a copy of the scene in the Pit. It also includes living animals (horses, aurochs, bisons and, perhaps one day, reindeers and ibex).

It is impossible to compare Lascaux and its reproduction. Let's just say that Lascaux II / Le Thot gives visitors more detailed information and is more accessible than anything they could have gleaned by visiting the real cave at Lascaux.

Brigitte and Gilles Delluc
U.A. 184, of the C.N.R.S.
Musée de l'Homme, Paris.

Bibliography

A few reference books

LEROI-GOURHAN Arl., ALLAIN J.and BALOUT L., BASSIER C., BOUCHEZ R., BOUCHUD J., COURAUD C., DELLUC B. and G., EVIN J., GIRARD M., LAMING-EMPERAIRE A., LEROI-GOURHAN A., ARRADET M., SCHWEIN-GRUBER F., TABORIN Y., VIALOU D., VOUVE J. (1979). **Lascaux inconnu**, 12th supplement to Gallia-Préhistoire, Ed. du C.N.R.S., Paris, 381 p, 387 fig. (the only scientific work dealing exclusively with the engravings and archaeology of the site).

LEROI-GOURHAN A. (1965, 1st ed.) **Préhistoire de l'Art occidental**, Mazenod (L'art et les grandes civilisations), Paris, 482 p, 739 ill. 804 fig. (1971, 2nd ed., revised and extended) (one chapter on the mural art in Lascaux).

LEROI-GOURHAN A. (1984) Grotte de Lascaux in **L'Art des cavernes** (Atlas archéologique de la France), Ministère de la Culture, Paris, p. 180-200, 30 fig.

A few works for the general public

DELLUC B. and G. (1984) **Lascaux. Art et archéologie**, Editions du Périgord Noir, Emmanuel Leymarie, Périgueux, 93 p., 18 fig., 4 pl., 4 plans.

DELLUC B. and G. (1985). **Tout Lascaux, petit journal**, single ed., Office du Tourisme de la Dordogne and Editions du Périgord Noir, Périgueux, 4 p., ill.

RUSPOLI M. with collab. of B.and G.DELLUC, H.de LUMLEY and M.PATOU (1986) **Lascaux, un nouveau regard**, Bordas, Paris, 207 p, ill.

A few specific subjects

BATAILLE G. (1955) **Lascaux ou la naissance de l'Art**, Skira, Geneva, 149 p., 68 ill., 6 inset pl. (1980, 2nd ed.), (attractively illustrated but the scientific bases on which Georges Bataille based his interesting text are now thirty years old and completely obsolete).

BRUNET J., MARSAL J., and VIDAL P. (1980) Lascaux. Où en sont les travaux de conservation ? **Archéologia**, No.149, pp.35-50, ill.

DELLUC B. and G. (1984) Lascaux II : copie conforme. **L'Histoire**, No. 64, pp. 76-79, 1 fig. (the creation of Lascaux II).

DELLUC B. and G. (1984) L'art pariétal avant Lascaux. **Dossiers Histoire et archéologie**, No. 87, pp. 52-60, 15 fig. (Lascaux' place in mural art of the Paleolithic Period).

DELLUC B. and G. (1990) **L'art préhistorique avant Lascaux**, supplement to Gallia-Préhistoire, Ed. du C.N.R.S., Paris (book in the press).

LEROI-GOURHAN Arl. (1980) Lascaux, **La Recherche**, Vol. 11, No. 110, pp.412-420, 6 fig. (brief description of the archaeology of Lascaux).

LEROI-GOURHAN Arl. (1982) L'archéologie de la grotte de Lascaux, **Pour la Science**, No. 58, pp.23-33, 12 fig.

VIALOU D. (1976) **Guide des grottes ornées paléolithiques ouvertes au public**, pub. Masson, Paris, 128 p., fig. (Lascaux' place among the decorated caves).

VIALOU D. (1984) Lascaux et l'art magdalénien, **Dossier Histoire et archéologie**, No.87, pp 61-69, 17 fig. (Lascaux' place in Paleolithic mural art).

VIALOU D. (1987) **L'art des cavernes. Les sanctuaires de la préhistoire.** Ed. du Rocher (Science and Discovery collection), 117 p., 28 fig. (Lascaux' place among decorated caves).

VOUVE J., BRUNET J., VIDAL P., MARSAL J. (1982) **Lascaux en Périgord noir**, pub. Fanlac, Périgueux, 87 p, ill (concentrates on problems of conservation).

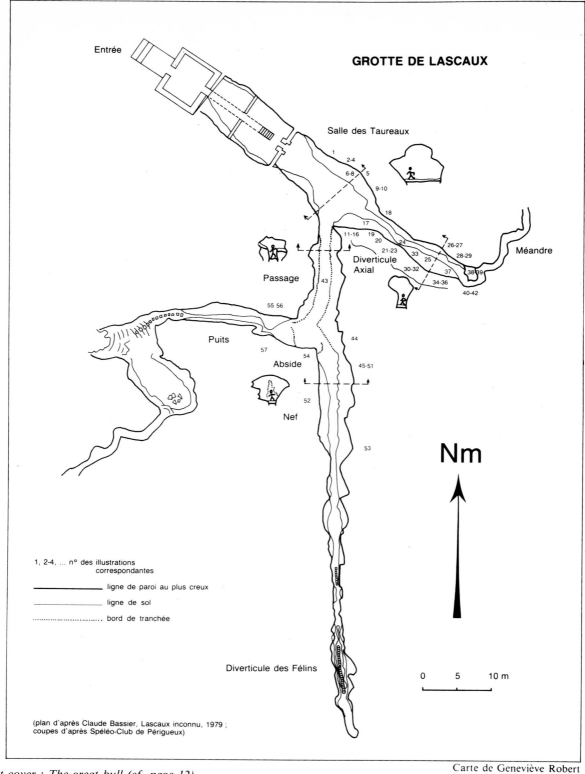

GROTTE DE LASCAUX

Entrée

Salle des Taureaux

Méandre

Diverticule Axial

Passage

Puits

Abside

Nef

Nm

1, 2-4, ... n° des illustrations
correspondantes

————— ligne de paroi au plus creux

————— ligne de sol

.... bord de tranchée

Diverticule des Félins

0   5   10 m

(plan d'après Claude Bassier, Lascaux inconnu, 1979 ;
coupes d'après Spéléo-Club de Périgueux)

Carte de Geneviève Robert

Front cover : The great bull (cf. page 12)
Back cover : The Well (cf. page 57).

© Copyright 1990 - Editions Sud Ouest. Ce livre a été imprimé par Pollina à Luçon (85) - France. La couverture a été tirée par l'imprimerie Raynard à La Guerche de Bretagne (35) , et pelliculée par Pollina.
ISBN : 2.9059.8382.5 - Editeur : 071.04.03.04.96 - N° d'impression : 69817 - B